# INSIDER TIPS FOR HUNTING SMALL GAME

XINA M. UHL AND
JUDY MONROE PETERSON

rosen publishing's
rosen
central®

New York

Published in 2019 by The Rosen Publishing Group, Inc.
29 East 21st Street, New York, NY 10010

First Edition

**Library of Congress Cataloging-in-Publication Data**

Names: Uhl, Xina M., author. | Peterson, Judy Monroe, author.
Title: Insider tips for hunting small game / Xina M. Uhl and Judy Monroe
Peterson.
Description: New York : Rosen Central, 2019. | Series: The ultimate guide
to hunting | Audience: Grades 5–8. | Includes bibliographical references and
index.
Identifiers: LCCN 2017048350| ISBN 9781508181804 (library bound) |
ISBN 9781508181811 (pbk.)
Subjects: LCSH: Small game hunting—Juvenile literature.
Classification: LCC SK340 .U35 2019 | DDC 799.2/5—dc23
LC record available at https://lccn.loc.gov/2017048350

*Manufactured in the United States of America*

# CONTENTS

# INTRODUCTION

In the United States and Canada, small game such as rabbits, squirrels, woodcocks, and quail are the most frequently hunted animals. Hunters find that North America affords easy access to these wild animals at a relatively low cost. Opportunities for hunting are available in many local, state, and federal lands. Hunting on private property may also be allowed at the discretion of the property owner.

Sometimes hunters must travel a few miles to access small game habitats. Rabbits are prolific breeders that can be found in every state and much of Canada. The same goes for squirrels. Upland birds like woodcocks and quails inhabit North America as well. In the fall, woodcocks can be hunted as they migrate from the northern states and Canada to southern locations. Quail inhabit the prairies, fields, and marshlands of many states.

Trips to hunt small wildlife can be made on short notice since they don't require much in the way of advance planning or expensive equipment. Because small animals are fast, cautious, and well adapted to their environment, finding and shooting these small targets is challenging and exciting. When hunters use their skills to hunt small game, they feel a sense of satisfaction and accomplishment, and if they are successful, they earn themselves healthy, delicious meat. In addition to hunting for the thrill of the chase and meat, some people use animal skins or display their quarry by having them mounted in their homes or hunting cabins. Small game hunting provides good mental and physical exercise since it is often necessary to walk long distances through an animal's habitat.

Wild rabbits, also called hares, live throughout North America. Cottontail rabbits are one of these. Jackrabbits are another, whose long ears make them easy to distinguish.

Spending time in nature, with its woods, fields, marshes, fresh air, and quiet brings enjoyment to many hunters. So does the opportunity to get away from the daily grind of work or school to hunt with friends and family, perhaps establishing a tradition. In some families, the older members teach the knowledge of hunting skills to the young people. It's easy to partner up with another hunter to search out small game and have fun in the meantime.

Hunting small game involves you in nature, giving you a chance to watch wildlife close up. Though hunting small game can be a challenge, it is a great choice for beginning hunters because it can be accomplished from sunrise to sundown during many months of the year. Woodcock and quail hunting season occurs for several months every fall.

Family members often pass their hunting knowledge and skills along to children, who in turn may pass them on to their descendants.

Licensed hunters play a large role in the management and conservation of wildlife. Animal habitats are increasingly destroyed by human intrusion, including construction of highways, houses, and farmland. The fees from hunting licenses and special taxes on hunting equipment provide money to the states to enforce hunting laws, manage wildlife, and maintain conservation programs.

Ultimately, though, small game is owned by the public. State and federal laws control hunting to avoid the overharvest and extinction of wild animals. If the population of one or more small game animals grows beyond its available food and shelter, laws are changed to allow an increased game harvest. Hunting seasons for each type of wild game is one means of managing wildlife populations since people can legally hunt only during the proper hunting season. All states have bag limits for each small game animal hunted, a limit that may change annually as a wildlife management tool. In addition to knowing the laws, hunters must also learn how to use their weapons, prepare for a hunt, and understand the behavior of small wildlife.

# CHAPTER ONE

# HUNTING BASICS

B ecoming a good hunter takes training, practice, and time. Good hunters are familiar with the habits and habitats of small game that live in fields and woods. They know how to handle their weapons with accuracy—and they never forget to be safe. Choosing the right weapons and ammunition for the type of game you are hunting not only makes the hunt more enjoyable, it also ups the chance it will succeed.

The purchase of hunting firearms is controlled by federal and state regulations. A hunter must be of legal age to buy a firearm for hunting. If a hunter is underage, an adult must buy and register the gun. Every state regulates the hunting season for each type of animal. The government also authorizes what firearms and archery can be used for hunting.

## SAFETY FIRST

States usually offer youth hunter education programs. These programs require beginning hunters to know and demonstrate safe weapon handling and shooting. During the course, beginning hunters learn to treat every firearm as if it is loaded. They are taught to keep the gun unloaded until they are actually hunting.

When carrying a gun while hunting, beginners learn to keep their fingers away from the trigger and to leave the safety switch on. The safety switch is a mechanical action that can fail, so hunters learn never to assume it is on. Firearms can shoot accidentally if the trigger pulls against brush or if the weapon falls to the ground.

When handling a gun, beginners are taught never to fire at sound or movement only or where hunters or other people might be. Although .22 caliber is small, bullets can easily travel up to 1 mile (1.6 kilometers). When shooting, hunters must always know what is behind the target. They should never shoot animals at the top of a hill or in a tree without a backstop because of the danger to people or property beyond the target. For their

Gun stores must follow state and federal firearm regulations closely in order to avoid trouble with the law.

own protection, hunters need to wear ear protectors and shooting glasses. Beginning hunters learn to store firearms and bullets in secure and separate places when not hunting or target shooting. Books and hunter training sites on the internet provide more information on safe hunting.

Safety is the highest priority for every hunter. Some hunters learn safety skills from family or friends who teach younger hunters. Other beginning hunters attend hunter education courses that are government sponsored. Local shooting or conservation clubs teach classes in archery and gun shooting and safety hunting skills. These hunter education courses cover small game identification, hunting regulations, and firearm and archery shooting and safe use.

Hunter safety classes teach hunters about proper ear and eye protection along with how to stand and position firearms and how to safely handle weapons.

Hunters have an ethical duty to shoot accurately and not wound a targeted small animal. Good hunters practice at shooting ranges to become skilled in the use of their gun or archery equipment. Some specialized shooting ranges have indoor and outdoor moving targets. Beginning hunters need to practice at targets placed at close ranges. They should practice shooting at longer ranges as their skills improve.

Shotguns require training and practice to consistently follow a target and shoot at the right moment to hit a flying bird. To practice shooting upland birds, the three main types of shotgun shooting at targets are skeet shooting, trapshooting, and sporting clays. Skeet shooting is shooting at clay pigeons (disks) that are flung into the air at high speed from different angles. In trap shooting, people shoot at clay pigeons that are thrown away from them in five different positions. Sporting clays is more difficult than trap or skeet because the targets are thrown many different distances and at many different angles, speeds, and heights. All three shotgun shooting methods are great ways to practice shooting in preparation for quail. Woodcock hunters tend to focus on skeet shooting for practice.

## BASICS OF SHOTGUNS AND MUZZLELOADERS

The shotgun is the only firearm used to hunt quail and woodcocks because after about 400 feet (122 meters), lead or steel shot loses power quickly and drops to the ground harmlessly. The shot is powerful at close range and spreads out in a pattern effective up to 100 feet (30 m). The expanding shot pattern provides multiple chances to harvest quail and woodcocks. Any gauge shotgun can be used for small game.

Many small game hunters prefer to use light loads with small lead shot because they increase the number of pellets that are aimed at the target.

Shotguns are available in five common gauges: .410 bore, 16 gauge, 20 gauge, 12 gauge, and 10 gauge. Although upland game birds are hunted with all gauges, the 12-gauge shotgun is the most popular. Beginning hunters might start with a .410 bore, 16-gauge, or 20-gauge to minimize the recoil. Actions for shotguns are the break open, bolt, pump, double barrel, and semiautomatic. Many quail and woodcock hunters prefer the 20-gauge double barrel or automatic for fast aiming and shooting.

Muzzleloaders that have smooth bores and are loaded with lead or steel shot are categorized as shotguns and can be legally used to hunt rabbits, squirrels, woodcocks, and quail in many areas. Hunting upland birds with muzzleloaders loaded with lead shot is challenging because a hunter can take only one shot with this type of gun. The reload requires one to two minutes. By then, the birds have flown out of shooting range.

## RIFLE BASICS

A common firearm used to shoot wild rabbits and squirrels is the .22 rifle. Many hunters choose this firearm because shots taken for small game are often within 50 feet (15 m). A .22 rifle has little or no recoil, or kickback. Young hunters should use a small-caliber rifle that fits the length of their arm.

Many small game hunters have a scope attached to the top of their rifle. To aim quickly, hunters line up the crosshairs (guides) inside the scope. Hunters can see an animal better because of the magnification of the scope. Scopes with lower power work best for close-range shooting of small game. A typical scope used

A scope helps hunters zero in on the game they are targeting, increasing accuracy and saving bullets as a result. Harvesting animals is also more efficient.

for small game is one-and-a-half times (1.5x) magnification. This means that an animal appears one-and-a-half times closer to the hunter. Small game hunting can also be successfully accomplished without a scope.

Hunters can select or use different bullets to find what works best when hunting small game. Different-powered bullets are available for the .22 rifle, including shorts, longs, and long rifles. Small game hunters can effectively use any of these cartridges. The most popular small game bullet is the .22-caliber long rifle. Hunters can find the caliber of a rifle stamped on its barrel. Some small game hunters prefer a combination gun with a .22-caliber barrel on top and a 20-gauge shotgun barrel on the bottom.

## BOW AND ARROW HANDLING

To hunt small game with a bow and arrow is difficult but rewarding. Compared to hunters using firearms, bowhunters must get closer to small wildlife to shoot accurately. The reason is simple: arrows do not travel as far as bullets. Shooting a bow and arrow is more difficult than shooting a firearm. Archers need to build up their shooting muscles and be able to concentrate and judge distances accurately. To successfully bowhunt, archers learn how to stand correctly and how to position their body and hands. An important skill for bowhunters is the precise placement of an arrow. Small, fast-moving animals present few chances to aim accurately. The key to being a good archer is the ability to relax and not force the arrow toward a target. This means that archers must wait for a sitting, stationary target. For safety, hunters should always inspect their bowstring before a hunt and replace frayed strings.

This young hunter is handling a compound bow. It is drawn back in a position that is ready for shooting.

Various rifle models with different actions are available. The most popular model for hunting small game is a bolt action, in which the bolt is operated by hand. Other rifle actions used are pump, break, semiautomatic, and lever. Hunters often choose an action depending on where and what small animal they will hunt.

# ARCHERY BASICS

Many hunters use archery when they begin hunting small game. Although any bow can be used to hunt squirrels and rabbits, many hunters prefer the compound bow. They can draw the arrow back and hold it while they wait for an animal to come into shooting range. They can do this because a compound bow reduces the amount of force needed to hold a bow that is ready for release. Bows are rated in pounds needed to pull the string back. For example, a bow rated at 30 pounds (14 kilograms) requires 30 pounds (14 kg) of force (strength) to pull back the string to draw an arrow. Bows with around 20 to 30 pounds (9–14 kg) of draw work well for harvesting small animals.

The blunt point arrow is preferred when hunting squirrels and rabbits. The arrow tip flairs, forming a wide striking surface. For squirrel hunting, blunt points are used with flu-flu arrows. Flu-flu is a type of arrow for short distance shooting. The feathers on flu-flu arrows are large. By using the blunt and flu-flu, bow-hunters can shoot accurately up to 50 feet (15 m). If an arrow misses the target, it falls harmlessly to the ground.

# CHAPTER TWO

# THINGS TO CONSIDER

**H**andling a weapon with the intent to kill an animal is a serious matter. All small game hunters have laws to follow and must take personal responsibility for their actions. Each state and province has its own regulations and laws designed to protect others, respect property rights, and control the harvest of available wildlife. The nation's land, water, and wildlife resources are not infinite, and they need to be treated as such by each hunter.

## THE NUMBER-ONE CONCERN

A hunting gun and bow are dangerous because of the power of bullets and arrows. Safety must be on the mind of every hunter at all times. Hunters need to be alert for and responsible to other people, including other hunters in the area. Every hunter needs to obey the laws regulating hunting and to respect the hunting area of others. The zone of fire is a term used for an area around a hunter where shooting can be done safely. When hunting alone, people can shoot in any direction at their small game target if they have a safe backstop to stop the bullet in the event that they miss.

16

Group hunting for small game such as rabbits and upland birds is fun and can be productive. However, it is important that the hunting partners always know the location of each other. Partners need to establish a zone of fire before they begin their hunt. Planning a group hunt increases hunting success and protects the safety of each partner. Sometimes, more than one hunter may harvest the same rabbit, woodcock, or other small game. When several hunters are responsible for the harvest, a decision must be made as to who takes possession of the animal. Group hunters may share equally in the number of animals harvested, or they may decide that the youngest hunter receives the prized animal.

## KEEP IT LEGAL

The harvest of small game animals is regulated by federal and state laws. Hunters must know and follow these rules. For example, hunters must buy a license to hunt squirrels, rabbits, quail, or woodcocks. They must know what type of gun or archery equipment can be used during each small game season. Regulations describe the number and type of small game. States set the months and days when each type of small game can be hunted legally.

States have bag limits for small game based on the available population for that animal. While in the field, hunters cannot have in their possession more than the daily bag limit for the target animal. Game wardens can stop hunters and ask to see how many small game animals are in their daily possession limit.

All states require that hunters have their hunting license and personal identification in their possession while hunting. This rule allows the positive identification of hunters if requested by law

Game wardens are important guardians of wilderness areas. This warden shown here looks out over the land in the Cody region near Meeteetse, Wyoming.

enforcement officials. Small game hunters renew their license every year, which is valid only for the season. All states have a detailed description of their hunting laws available in free booklets or on each state department of natural resources' website.

## BE ETHICAL

Ethical hunters behave according to what is right. Ethics are personal decisions beyond what federal or state laws require. When

## MIGRATORY BIRD HARVEST INFORMATION PROGRAM

Every season, people who hunt woodcocks and other migratory game birds are required to be licensed with the Migratory Bird Harvest Information Program (HIP). The U.S. Fish & Wildlife Service and state wildlife agencies jointly run this program. The purpose of HIP is to increase the accuracy of harvest estimates of migratory birds. This information is used to help wildlife managers make decisions concerning hunting seasons, bag limits, and population management. People must buy a license to hunt migratory birds in each state they do so. They are also required to buy a HIP permit. The permit might be a card, stamp, or other item, and it must be renewed each year. The procedures to sign up for HIP vary from state to state. Hunters must carry proof of their HIP license with them when hunting migratory birds. You can learn more about the program by visiting the U.S. Fish & Wildlife website.

a hunter is fair and polite to other hunters, other people encountered, and personal property, good ethics is the result. Proper behavior while hunting is a personal code. This set of behavioral standards is termed the hunter's code, and it is as important as hunting regulations.

Here is an example of ethical behavior when hunting upland birds. When dogs point at hiding birds, beginning hunters or hunters who have not taken any game can move to the most likely flushing zones. This action increases their chance for a successful shot. Sometimes an ethical hunting decision might involve two people who want to hunt the same area for small

Dogs have been used by hunters for thousands of years. In fact, hunting is one of the main reasons that dogs became domesticated in the first place.

game. Instead of arguing, they might decide to share the location or alternate the days that each hunter is at that spot. Poachers are unethical people who hunt illegally. They might break small game laws by going over their bag limit or hunt without a license and harvest small game. They might harvest wildlife outside of its season or during the season without following the regulations. When caught, poachers are fined and lose their hunting privileges. Hunting weapons and vehicles are often seized and not returned.

## ENTERING HUNTING LANDS

Small game animals live wild lives, with no respect to human-made boundaries. However, hunters must know where it is legal to hunt them. They need to avoid trespassing on private property, which means they always need to know their location. Hunting without permission on private land that has posted No Trespassing or No Hunting signs is a crime.

It may be tempting to ignore posted signs, but it could have costly consequences, including fines and other law enforcement actions.

Landowners need to be approached for permission to hunt on their land. Private land with farm animals, equipment, and farmland must be treated carefully by hunters. On completion of the hunt, it is appropriate for hunters to say a genuine "thank you" to the landowner. If a hunt is successful, many hunters share their game with the landowners. In repayment for the privilege of hunting on private land, hunters will often help the landowner with a special project. Farmers, for example, might need labor during certain seasons of farming, such as putting up hay, building fences, or helping with the harvest. Most landowners will allow helpful and respectful hunters to return for additional hunts.

The government owns public land, including national forests and state wildlife management areas. Hunting on public property for small game requires hunters to treat the land and public campgrounds with respect. For instance, hunters should clear and carry away their own and other litter in the area during their hunt.

# LOOKING GOOD FOR THE PUBLIC

Many people enjoy being outdoors and watching wildlife. Responsible hunters make certain that their actions are not offensive. Some nonhunters are afraid of hunting firearms or develop antihunting opinions based on the behavior of irresponsible hunters. Hunters carrying guns and archery equipment should present a positive image and use common sense and courtesy. To be respectful, hunters in public settings should store unloaded guns in cases and out of sight when they are not in use.

Hunters who do not take unfair advantage of small game animals are practicing "fair chase." An example of an unfair chase is if a person in a vehicle drives, herds, or takes any rabbits or upland birds from a moving vehicle or boat under motor power. Responsible hunters know their guns or archery equipment, how they function, and how to not wound their target. If an animal is wounded, hunters should try to track and recover it. Responsible hunters often help each other during recovery. For a hunter to become an accurate shot and not wound an animal, it is necessary that the hunter have lots of target practice.

After small game is harvested, hunters have a duty to use the meat. They can share the meat with nonhunters. Successful hunters often photograph or preserve their harvested animals. As hunters travel to and from hunting areas, they should cover or put their harvested animals in coolers so they do not offend nonhunters.

# ENSURING WILDLIFE HAVE A HOME

Wildlife conservation programs sponsored by the government guarantee a healthy wildlife population. Sometimes a particular wildlife population becomes too small and could become extinct. When this happens, the animal is endangered and cannot be hunted by law. As cities, road systems, and farmland become larger, the natural habitat of animals is often destroyed. The populations of small game animals may decrease. Hunting clubs and associations work with nonhunting organizations to encourage a healthy wildlife population. Together they buy large areas of wild land where small game can live and thrive. Responsible hunters support healthy wildlife populations by following the legal hunting season and harvesting only the allowable number of animals.

Nonhunters and hunters must continue to work together to guarantee stable wildlife populations for future generations. For example, rabbit populations often boom every nine to eleven years. If they get too large, the animals cannot find enough food. They might eat most or all of certain plants in an area. Without enough food, the rabbit populations will starve. They might get sick and infect other wild animals with disease. Hunters help by thinning or reducing small animals like rabbits from overpopulating an area.

# CHAPTER THREE

# PLANNING A TRIP

One of the best aspects of small game hunting is the chance to spend time outdoors and become acquainted with the natural world that can seem so far removed from many city dwellers. First, though, hunters have a number of decisions to make, such as where to hunt. Hunters may live in an area with a large population of small game, or they may have to research a place to find them. Before leaving on a trip, it's a good idea to take some time to study small animals in their environment and practice outdoor skills.

## WHERE TO HUNT?

Finding a place to hunt is an important step in planning. Wild-life managers and conservation officers can tell hunters where to get any necessary reservations and permits. These officials sometimes know farmers or ranchers who would like hunters to reduce the numbers of rabbits or squirrels on their land. Beginners can ask more experienced hunters or members of a hunting group for suggestions. If a good hunting spot is on private property, hunters can check the websites of the office of the local assessor or county to find the owner. Public land, such as national forests, is often open to hunting. Hunters should check with the U.S. Forest Service about hunting on public lands.

People must contact the owner of private land and ask permission to hunt for a particular small game animal. To scout, or look at, the area, hunters should contact the landowner before

This person uses a compass and a topographic map to accurately find a good hunting location near Martinsville, Indiana.

hunting season begins. Scouting helps hunters learn about an area and its wildlife. Topographic and aerial maps also provide information useful to someone unfamiliar with a particular area.

## UNDERSTANDING ANIMAL BEHAVIOR

To increase the chance of finding and shooting small animals, hunters need to understand the animals and their habitats. Small game animals live where they have plant food and shelter. They do not travel far. However, woodcocks migrate great distances. When hunters find where wildlife feed or rest, their success at harvest increases. Small wild animals have keen senses of sight and hearing, which alert them to danger. Squirrels, rabbits, quail, and woodcocks react quickly by fleeing or hiding when hunters come too close.

## LEARNING ABOUT RABBITS

The most harvested types of rabbits in the United States are cottontail and snowshoe. Cottontails live across much of the United States except the far west and are also found in areas of southern Canada. From nose to fluffy, white tail, they measure fourteen to nineteen inches (thirty-six to forty-eight centimeters) and weigh 2 to 4 pounds (0.9–1.8 kg). They prefer to live in forests with open areas nearby, heavy brush, and tall grasses. They eat green plants. If food is in short supply, they will chew the twigs and bark of trees and shrubs.

Although the snowshoe rabbit is really a hare, it is usually called a rabbit. Its winter-white fur changes to brown in the summer. Snowshoes live in most of the forests of the northern United States, Alaska, and south along the Rocky and Appalachian mountains and in much of Canada. They prefer thick brush underneath trees. A little larger than cottontails, snowshoes are about 18 inches (46 cm) in length and weigh 3 to 4 pounds (1.4–1.8 kg). They eat the bark of trees and shrubs and also twigs, grasses, and other plants.

## BASICS ABOUT SQUIRRELS

Hunters usually harvest two types of squirrels for meat: gray squirrels and fox squirrels. Gray squirrels live in the eastern half of the United States and in several regions of the West, as well as southern parts of Canada. They weigh about 1.5 pounds (680 grams) and are about 18 inches (46 cm) in length, which includes their big, bushy tail. Gray squirrels prefer hardwood trees (trees with broad leaves) or mixed forests with nut trees like oak, hickory, beech, pecan, and walnut. They live in tree holes or build nests in trees. They are active year round. Larger than gray squirrels, fox squirrels measure 19 to 30 inches (48–76 cm) long and weigh up to 3 pounds (1.4 kg). They inhabit the same eastern area of the United States as gray squirrels, but they range slightly more to the west. These prefer large hardwood trees, borders of cypress swamps, and thick grasses or bushes.

Squirrels are frisky and intelligent animals. They eat nuts, seeds, some fruits, insects, and bird eggs. They also like the buds, leaves, and young leaves of trees. In the fall, gray squirrels store away nuts and seeds for the winter. They place them in hollow logs, in holes in trees, or under leaves. They later find them with their keen sense of smell. Fox squirrels spend most of their waking time looking for nuts and other food.

Squirrels are found in many areas throughout North America. They are frequently seen as pests who raid bird feeders and store nuts in chimneys.

## WHAT ARE WOODCOCKS?

Woodcock is the name of several types of birds that live in moist woods, near streams, lowland pasture regions with tall grass,

Woodcocks can be hard to locate due to their excellent camouflage. At dawn and dusk, however, the males give loud calls and perform flying displays in an effort to win mates.

and in sheltered wet areas. This land includes stands of alder, aspen, birch, and poplar trees along the banks of streams, beaver ponds, and marshes. Hunters focus on the American woodcock, which appears east of the Mississippi River and north to southern

Canada. The woodcock is a migratory bird. Flying at night in short hops, woodcocks usually follow the same routes south and north each year. They winter from New Jersey to Missouri and south to the Gulf Coast and then fly north in late February or early March to nest and raise their chicks. Adult birds measure about 11 inches (28 cm) long and have a chunky body and short legs and wings. They use their long bill to probe the mud for earthworms and grubs (soft, thick, wormlike larvae of certain beetles). They also eat insects, weed seeds, and berries. Because their eyes are set far back on their head, they can easily see danger. The woodcock is mostly tan and brown. These colors camouflage the bird in its habitat of wood and dead leaves and help protect it from enemies.

## ABOUT QUAILS

Five types of quails are usually hunted in the United States: bobwhite, California, Gambel's, scaled, and mountain.

California quails are found in oak woodlands, sagebrush, chaparral and foothill forests. They can also live near people in parks and gardens.

An important game bird, bobwhites live year round in most of the eastern half of the United States up to southern Minnesota and South Dakota and in eastern Washington and Oregon. They eat mostly seeds of grass and weeds and also feed on grains in farmlands, acorns, insects, and berries. They roost (sleep or rest) along wooded streams, the edges of woods, and wet, grassy areas. Bobwhites average about 10 inches (25 cm) in length and 8 ounces (227 g) in weight. Fast runners, they seldom fly. If in danger, they will fly short distances up to 30 miles per hour (48 km/h).

The California quail's range is through the Pacific states, and the Gambel's and scaled quails inhabit the American Southwest. All three birds prefer semiarid desert brush areas. The largest of all the quails, the mountain quail mostly resides in the Pacific states. They live in higher locations with lots of oak trees and short grass. The Gambel's, scaled, and mountain quail eat weed and brush seeds.

# GETTING IN SHAPE

Sometimes hunters walk long distances, so being in good physical condition is important for an enjoyable hunt. Hunters must be prepared for unexpected situations or emergencies when they are scouting or hunting. It is important that hunters always tell someone where they are going and when they expect to return. Outdoor skills are necessary for hunters. For example, hunters should know how to build a fire and signal for help if that becomes necessary.

Besides their shotgun or bow, hunters often bring other items, including a small knife. Binoculars help them look for small game and identify legal small game animals. They carry a compass or use a global positioning system (GPS). Hunters may want to carry their phones, in case they have to make emergency calls. Many states require hunters to wear blaze orange clothing so that other hunters can see them. Even if not required by law to do so, hunters might wear blaze orange vests and hats. Many squirrel hunters wear camouflage clothing, which helps to keep animals from seeing them in the woods. It is a good idea for hunters to wear outdoor gear, such as waterproof boots, brush pants, and a jacket that does not catch on burrs.

# CHAPTER FOUR

# APPROACHES TO HUNTING

One style of hunting does not work for all types of small game and all seasons or terrains. Because of this, small game hunters can approach different types of hunts in the most suitable manner for the conditions. Hunters must adjust their plans according to the size of their hunting parties, the weapons they will be using, the weather, and the type of terrain where they are hunting. Hunters must learn the wind direction if they are hunting woodcocks or quail. And they must also know how sensitive small game is to strange scents, noises, or movements from hunters since hiding is often their best defense from danger.

## PURSUING RABBITS

Most rabbit hunting is usually done with one or two people. Single hunters typically jump shoot rabbits. In this method, they slowly move through thick grass or brush and look for hiding places of rabbits, such as brush piles or windblown trees. Shelter belts also make excellent homes for small game animals, especially rabbits. These strips of trees and bushes are planted around farmland to reduce the erosion of the soil caused by heavy rain or wind. When hunters get close, the hidden rabbit jumps up, runs about 100 feet (30 m), and then stops. While the rabbit is running, hunters stand still at the hiding place. Once

Dogs bred to hunt are trained not to bite hard into the prey they retrieve for hunters. This is called having a soft mouth and can be a hard skill to teach dogs.

the rabbit stops, the hunters pick up a viable target of the animal and make the harvest. A single hunter might use a dog to hunt. Then the hunter and dog slowly move through a rabbit's habitat.

When a rabbit jumps out of its hiding place, the hunter sends the dog on the animal's track. The hunter stays where the rabbit was jumped. The rabbit runs quickly to escape as the dog chases it. A rabbit pushed hard by a dog will run a long distance. However, it will run in a large circle, usually back to where it was jumped. When the rabbit returns, the hunter can harvest it.

Rabbit hunting is also done in small groups. One person rattles the hiding place with sticks or jumps on the hiding place, scaring the rabbit out so that the partner can harvest it. Another way is for one hunter to quickly walk after the moving rabbit, while the other hunter stays where the rabbit was jumped. A scared rabbit will run in a large circle and then will return to its home shelter, where the hunter may be able to shoot it.

Rabbit hunting is especially successful with a snow cover on the ground. Rabbits live and feed in a small area of about five acres (two hectares). When hunters find rabbit tracks in the snow, they know the animals are close and hunting in that spot may be productive. Rabbits tend to run on the same game trail, making paths in the snow. Skillful hunters look for this type of rabbit trail in the snow and then hunt in the area. All methods of rabbit hunting lend themselves to the .22 rifle, small-gauge shotguns, and bows and arrows. In many states, rabbit hunting season opens in late summer and continues until February or March.

## GOING AFTER SQUIRRELS

Successful squirrel hunting depends on finding a stand of trees where they feed and rest. A stand of oak trees produces acorns, which are the favorite food of squirrels. If acorns are in short supply, they eat other kinds of nuts. Because squirrels blend in well with their surroundings, they may be difficult to see, especially if leaves are on the trees. Squirrels are also good at hiding and move quickly from tree to tree.

Squirrel hunting season typically opens in late summer and continues to February. Many states have a summer hunting season. Hunters search for squirrels in trees. Early in the season, the animals only go to the ground to pick up acorns and other seeds that have fallen. They spend more time on the ground to gather, dig, and store nuts later in the season. To find where squirrels feed, hunters look for piles of small pieces of

Hunters often conceal themselves against trees in an effort to keep prey from spotting them.

chewed nuts and shells under trees. In light snow or mud, hunters can easily see where squirrels have been scratching through the snow or leaves to retrieve nuts and seeds.

The most common squirrel hunting method is to walk slowly through the woods on a day without much wind. Hunters listen for the sounds of leaves rustling and squirrels chattering to locate the animals. Squirrels are not sensitive to human odor, but they have excellent vision. They can detect movement far before hunters know squirrels are in the area. Once hunters find a good spot, they sit quietly against a tree and look for squirrels. Otherwise, they use a tool called a squirrel call to chatter back to the squirrel. The call and lack of movement soon relaxes the alerted squirrels. They will start feeding again, presenting excellent targets. Many times, several squirrels in an area can be called in over a short period of time. Sometimes a hunter tosses a stick or rock on one side of the tree and then slips quickly to the other side. The motion frightens squirrels over to the side of the hunter.

When squirrel hunting, archers use flu-flu arrows so that the arrow drops to the ground after 50 feet (15 m). Because .22-caliber bullets can travel 1 mile (1.61 km), squirrel hunters must have a backstop, which is usually a tree branch or trunk or a hill behind a tree. If the hunter's shot misses an animal, the bullet will lodge harmlessly in a backstop. Shotgun and muzzleloader lead shot are very dangerous at close range, although after 500 feet (152 m), they pose little danger. Safe hunters must make sure that their shot at the target does not hit any livestock, people, or equipment behind it.

# WOODCOCK HUNTING TIPS

Early fall is the time to hunt woodcocks. Then the birds are flying on their migratory routes, going from their northern home to their southern home. Hunters look for areas with moist or wet soil or shallow standing pools of water where migrating woodcocks like to feed. They also search for whitewash, or droppings,

# DIFFERENT SQUIRREL-HUNTING TECHNIQUES

Some people successfully hunt squirrels with a dog, which will search back and forth on the ground for the animals. Upon finding a squirrel, the barking dog chases it into a tree and then sits by the tree until the hunter arrives. The hunter usually finds the squirrel on the opposite side of the tree from the dog. Two other squirrel hunting methods can be productive. One is to team hunt with a partner. A squirrel typically hides on the opposite side of a tree trunk to get away from a hunter. By team hunting, a squirrel cannot hide on the other side of the tree without being seen by the hunters. Another method is to float hunt in canoes or flat-bottom boats along streams bordered by nut trees. Squirrels like to be close to water and will live in the nut trees, such as oak, that line a stream's banks.

Hunting with a partner can be an effective means of nabbing small game, but only if you coordinate your actions with one another.

on the ground where the birds have been feeding. Woodcocks tend to come to feeding areas an hour before sunset.

A dog is needed to flush woodcocks because the birds hold very tight. Hunters can nearly walk on them before they flush. Different kinds of dogs can be effective when hunting wood-cocks. Some hunters use pointers to flush the birds. Retriever dogs find wounded or harvested woodcocks.

Hunters shoot woodcocks as they rise or just before they level off into the air. Otherwise, the birds weave and dart in the air, making them a difficult target. When woodcocks are flushed, they fly about 50 to 75 yards (46–69 m) and then land. If flushed again, the birds repeat their flying and landing pattern. If hunters miss their target the first time, they can probably try to follow and shoot again. Many states allow only two to four woodcocks per day during the season.

# QUAIL BEHAVIOR

Quail hunting season varies by state, but it is often in the fall. Quail are regularly found in a covey (group) along brushy strips of land, such as fence lines, ditch lines, railroad tracks, or shelter belts. Hunters look for a circle of droppings to locate quail because they sleep back to back as a covey in a circle to conserve warmth and guard against predators. They tend to use the same spot for several nights. Individual hunters usually walk slowly toward the birds to flush a covey of quail. A group of two or three partners can be effective. The hunters fan out in a line and slowly walk through quail habitat, hoping to jump the birds and get multiple shots. Most hunters will shoot the birds as they flush but refrain from chasing the singles, which allows the unharvested birds to regroup.

The only firearm used to hunt quail is the shotgun. The most common shotguns are the 12 and 20 gauge with lead or steel shot ranging from size 4 to 8. It is important that a hunter picks a single bird to shoot because shooting at a covey seldom brings down a bird. Quail are shot in the air. All kinds of dogs can be effective in hunting quail. Pointing dogs cover more ground and hold the birds until hunters can get into position to shoot. Retrievers, such as the springer spaniel, are better at flushing and retrieving wounded or harvested birds. Compared to pointers, flushers and retrievers work closer to the hunters. They may be more effective when birds are not holding (staying in their hiding place), as the hunters are more likely to be closer to the flush.

# CHAPTER FIVE

# WHEN THE HUNT IS OVER

**H**unters who manage to harvest small game cannot rest easy when they have brought the animal down. As soon as possible, they must retrieve the animal and then dress it, or remove the intestines and internal organs. Speedy processing of downed animals helps to ensure healthy, safe, tasty meat. After an animal has been dressed, it can be moved to the hunter's camp or residence. The hunter may butcher, or cut up, the animal into smaller pieces or pay a professional to do it. Butchering requires several items of basic equipment: latex gloves, a sharp pocket knife, sealable plastic bags, and paper towels for cleanup.

After the animal is dressed, it is left whole for roasting or cut into smaller pieces for cooking. People use a sharp knife or game shears (scissors) to cut up the meat. Next, hunters remove any pellets, shot, or BBs in the meat. After the meat is washed in cold water, it is ready to be cooked or frozen for later use. Plastic bags with locking seals are an excellent way to safely freeze small game meat. Small game meat is delicious, lean, and can be cooked in many ways.

These hunters have been successful at harvesting small game, but even unsuccessful hunting trips can be enjoyable because of time spent in nature.

# DECORATION OR DISPLAY

Some hunters skin their squirrels or rabbits to tan their hides. The hides can be used to trim gloves and other clothing. People might use or sell squirrel hides and tails for making artificial flies (trout fishing bait). Sometimes they will take a hide to a taxidermist to be preserved and mounted for display. This professional starts by covering a premade foam model of the squirrel or rabbit with special glue. Then the tanned hide of the animal is carefully stretched and fitted on the model. Glass eyes are then glued into

Processing your harvest quickly is a good way of ensuring that the meat does not spoil, causing sickness.

place. After the glue dries, the squirrel or rabbit is ready to be put on display in a special place in a home or cabin. Schools and science museums often have mounted animals for study.

## PROCESSING RABBIT

When the temperature is warm, it is critical to dress rabbits in the field to quickly cool the meat. Hunters field dress a rabbit by first putting the animal on its back. They slit the underside up to the neck and remove the intestines and internal organs. Then they clean the cavity with paper towels, leaves, or snow.

Skinning a rabbit can be done in the field or at camp or home. Hunters have different methods for skinning the animal. One way is to pinch the hide up and away from the middle of the spine. Next, they cut the hide from the spine down the sides, being careful not to cut the meat. With both hands, they hold and pull the hide in opposite directions so that the legs are skinned up to the feet. Then hunters remove the feet, head, and tail.

To prepare rabbit for cooking, people usually cut the front legs from the body at the shoulder. After that, they cut and remove the hind legs at the hip. They separate the rib section from the loin and cut the back into two or three pieces, depending on the size of the animal. Because the rib cage does not have much meat, hunters remove it. They might use the rib cage and front legs to make soup.

## DRESSING SQUIRRELS

Squirrels must be dressed and skinned after shooting. If the temperature is warm, the meat can begin to spoil quickly. Hunters often dress harvested squirrels in the field. To begin, they flip the animal onto its back. Using a sharp knife, they cut the underside of the tail and the tailbone. Then they cut around the squirrel's middle and step on the tail near the body. While the tail is held down, they pull the rear legs up and peel the skin up and off. Next, the front legs are cut off, the skin is removed, and the head is cut off. Finally, the back legs are removed and the remaining skin is pulled off.

Next, hunters flip the squirrel over so that its belly is up. They carefully cut down the rib cage through the pelvic bone (front part of the hip bone). As they cut, hunters take care not to nick the stomach and intestines. Once the animal's back legs are spread open, the intestines and internal organs are pulled out, and the cavity of the animal is wiped clean with paper towels, leaves, or snow. Then the legs are cut off and placed into cold water. The ribs are cut off next and discarded with parts such as the intestines, skin, head, and tail. Hunters typically cut the animal into five or six pieces: two front legs, two back legs, and one or two back pieces.

## ILLNESS FROM SMALL GAME

People can get sick from processing rabbits infected with tularemia, a disease caused by the bacterium *Francisella tularensis*. The bacterium can enter through the butcher's skin, eyes, or mouth. To be safe, wise hunters wear latex gloves while dressing, skinning, or butchering animals. The gloves can be found in the personal medical or pharmacy section of most general retail stores. Outdoor and hunting supply stores also carry them. While processing, people should not touch their mouth or eyes. When they are finished, many hunters put their gloves and discarded animal parts into plastic bags and seal them. Then they put the bags into the trash so that pet cats and dogs cannot reach them. Next, they wash their hands well, even if they wore latex gloves. To reduce the risk of spoilage, hunters immediately chill small game meat by putting it into a cooler with ice or a refrigerator or freezer.

## HOW TO PROCESS QUAIL AND WOODCOCK

If the weather is warm, hunters often dress upland birds in the field soon after they are shot. In cool weather, many people wait until they are at their vehicle, camp, or home. If the birds are not field dressed, hunters put them into a cloth bag or a hunting vest with a large pocket on the back. Others clip the birds to their belt. Once home, they skin the bird or pluck the feathers. Some people leave the skin on to help keep the small birds moist during cooking. Next, the wings and neck are cut from the body and discarded. The legs are snipped off just above the ankle joint. After the birds are cleaned under cold running water, they are patted dry and are now ready to cook or to be packaged and frozen.

## TIME FOR EATING

The meat of small game is lean, meaning it has little fat. Squirrel meat is dark, and rabbit meat is white. The age of an animal affects the texture and taste, which in turn affects the cooking methods. Young squirrels and rabbits usually have tender meat, while older animals may have tougher meat. Bobwhite quail meat is a light color, and the average dressed weight is 6 ounces (170 g). Woodcock has both white and dark meat with an average dressed weight of 5 ounces (142 g). Light meat is drier than dark meat and usually cooks faster.

People cook squirrels, rabbits, and small game birds in many ways, including roasting, grilling, broiling, baking, frying, or smoking. The meat can also be prepared in other healthy ways, such as in soups, stews, and casseroles. Cooking squirrels, rabbits, or game birds slowly in an electric Crock-Pot with vegetables and broth or another liquid provides a simple but great meal.

## BEFORE YOU HUNT AGAIN

Before leaving the area, hunters should thank the other hunters and private landowners who helped in the successful harvest. It is a good idea to offer to share small game meat with the landowner and with relatives or nonhunting friends. Even if the hunt did not produce results, the landowner should be thanked for the use of the private land.

Few things are as delicious and satisfying as meat cooked over an open fire.

Preparation for the next hunt begins as soon as hunters come home. They should clean and safely store their firearm or archery. Hunters' success at small game hunting increases as their skills improve. Small game hunters can apply these skills to other types of hunting, such as big game or varmint hunting.

Small game hunters have many opportunities to refine their hunting skills. They can sign up with a club to learn how to shoot expertly. They can join an outdoor off-season club to help with habitat or conservation management. Members in other organizations can teach small game hunters other skills, such as how to use a GPS system for location. To learn more about animal behavior, hunters can study at natural history museums or zoos. Books and magazines are available to help people learn more about guns, ammunition, hunting dogs, game calls, and archery equipment that can be used in future hunts. A great way to learn the sport of small game hunting is to help a friend become a good hunter.

# GLOSSARY

**ammunition** Bullets and gunpowder used in firearms.

**archery** The skill of shooting with a bow and arrow.

**bag limit** The number of a particular type of animal that a hunter can harvest during a day.

**barrel** The metal tube of a rifle.

**butcher** To process an animal's meat into usable sizes.

**caliber** The inside diameter of the barrel of a rifle or the diameter of a bullet.

**camouflage** Anything that conceals a person or equipment by making them appear to be part of the natural surroundings.

**conservation** Protection and preservation of nature.

**dress** To prepare a recently harvested animal so that its body temperature lowers and the meat stays fresh.

**endangered** An animal population in such small numbers that it is in danger of becoming extinct.

**ethics** A set of moral principles.

**extinction** No longer existing.

**flush** To cause a hidden bird to fly away suddenly.

**game** Wild animals hunted for food or sport.

**global positioning system (GPS)** Handheld computers that can calculate an exact position using a global positioning satellite.

**habitat** The area or environment where an animal lives.

**harvest** The act of shooting and recovering an animal.

**illegal** Against the law.

**migrate** To move from one location to another every season.

**pelvic bone** The bone on the front part of the hip.

**poacher** A person who takes game in a forbidden area or game that is illegal to take.

**possession limit** The maximum number of a type of animal that can be in a hunter's possession at any time.

**prolific** Abundant.

**quarry** An animal pursued in hunting.

**safety** A device on a firearm that keeps it from being fired.

**scope** A small telescope on a rifle barrel.

**season** The length of time to hunt specific game.

**tanning** A process by which animal hides are cleaned and preserved for clothing or other uses.

**target** Something that is aimed at to shoot by firearms or bow and arrow.

**varmint** An animal that destroys property, carries disease, or puts human or animal lives at risk.

# FOR MORE INFORMATION

Canadian Parks and Wilderness Society
506-250 City Centre Avenue
Ottawa, ON K I R 6K7
Canada
(800) 333-9453
Website: http://www.cpaws.org
Facebook and Twitter: @cpaws
Instagram: @cpaws_national
A Canadian charity dedicated to protecting public land, water, and
    wildlife. It has aided in the protection of more than half a million
    square kilometers in more than fifty years.

International Hunter Education Association (IHEA)
800 East 73rd Avenue, Unit 2
Denver, CO 80229
(303) 430-7233
Website: http://www.ihea-usa.org
Facebook: @InternationalHunterEducationAssociation
IHEA's mission is "to continue the heritage of hunting world-
    wide by developing safe, responsible, knowledgeable and
    involved hunters."

National Bowhunter Education Foundation
PO Box 2934
Rapid City, SD 57709
(605) 716-0596
Website: http://www.nbef.org
This organization provides bowhunting education and classes
    across the United States, including the National Archery in
    the Schools Program (NASP).

National Rifle Association of America
11250 Waples Mill Road
Fairfax, VA 22030
(800) 672-3888
Website: http://www.nra.org
Facebook and Twitter: @NRA
Instagram: @nationalrifleassociation
The National Rifle Association of America provides firearms
education and advocacy throughout the world.

Parks Canada National Office
30 Victoria Street
Gatineau, Quebec J8X 0B3
Canada
(888) 773-8888
Website: https://www.pc.gc.ca/en
Facebook and Twitter: @ParksCanada
Instagram: @parks.canada
This government agency is committed to protecting both the nat-
ural and cultural heritage of Canada's wilderness and territory
in a way that ensures the health of human and animal species.

U.S. Fish & Wildlife Service
1849 C Street NW
Washington, DC 20240
(800) 344-9453
Website: http://www.fws.gov
Facebook, Twitter, and Instagram: @usfws
This government agency manages the United States' natural
resources in order to conserve, protect, and enhance
wildlife, plants, and their habitats.

USDA Forest Service
Attn: Office of Communication
Mailstop: 1111
1400 Independence Avenue SW
Washington, DC 20250-1111
(800) 832-1355
Website: http://www.fs.fed.us
Facebook: @USForestService
Twitter: @forestservice
Instagram: @u.s.forestservice
An agency of the US Department of Agriculture, the Forest Service manages and maintains millions of acres of public lands in national forests and grasslands.

# FOR FURTHER READING

Carpenter, Tom. *Small-Game Hunting*. Minneapolis, MN : Abdo Publishing, 2016.

Gaspar, Joe, and Jack Weaver. *Hunting*. New York, NY: Rosen Publishing, 2016.

Graubart, Norman D. *How to Track a Rabbit*. New York, NY: Windmill Books, 2015.

Gurtler, Janet. *Small Game*. New York, NY: AV2 by Weigl, 2016.

Hemstock, Annie. *Bow Hunting*. New York, NY: Rosen Publishing, 2015.

Kuhn, Todd A. *Shooter's Bible Guide to Bowhunting*. New York, NY: Skyhorse Publishing, 2013.

Milner, Robert. *Absolutely Positively Gundog Training: Positive Training for Your Retriever Gundog*. CreateSpace, 2015.

Nickens, T. Edward. *The Best of the Total Outdoorsman: 501 Essential Tips and Tricks*. San Francisco, CA: Weldon Owen, 2017.

Tabor, Thomas C. *Shooter's Bible Guide to the Hunting Rifle and Its Ammunition*. New York, NY: Skyhorse Publishing, 2013.

Trisler, Dennis. *101 Squirrel Hunting Tips (& a few ways to cook 'em)*. Hermitage, TN: Stone River Press, 2014.

# BIBLIOGRAPHY

Boddington, Craig. *Fair Chase in North America*. Missoula, MT: Boone & Crockett Club, 2004.

Brakefield, Tom. *Small Game Hunting*. Philadelphia, PA: J. B. Lippincott Company, 1978.

Byers, Joe. *The Ultimate Guide to Crossbow Hunting: How to Successfully Bowhunt Big and Small Game Across North America*. New York, NY: Skyhorse Publishing, 2016.

Editors of Creative Publishing. *Dressing and Cooking Wild Game*. Chanhassen, MN: Creative Publishing, 2000.

Ellman, Robert. *The Game Bird Hunter's Bible*. New York, NY: Doubleday, 1993.

Geer, Galen. *Meat on the Table: Modern Small-Game Hunting*. Boulder, CO: Paladin Press, 1985.

Gunnersden.com. "Small Game Hunting." Retrieved December 5, 2017. http://www.gunnersden.com/index.htm.hunting -small-game.html.

Harrington, Dan. (Woodcock Hunter, Spooner, WI) in discussion with the author, February 2010.

Hehner, Mike, Chris Dorsey, and Greg Breining. *North American Game Birds*. Minnetonka, MN: Cy Decosse, 1996.

Lawrence, H. Lea. *The Ultimate Guide to Small Game and Varmint Hunting: How to Hunt Squirrels, Rabbits, Hares, Woodchucks, Coyotes, Foxes and More*. Guilford, CT: Lyons Press, 2002.

Lemke, Chris. (Outdoor Connection, Two Harbors, MN) in discussion with the author, February 2010.

Maas, David R. *North American Game Animals*. Minnetonka, MN: Cy Decosse, 1995.

Meili, Launi. *Rifle: Steps to Success*. Champaign, IL: Human Kinetics, 2008.

Minnesota Department of Natural Resources, Division of Law Enforcement. *Minnesota Firearms Safety Hunter Education,*

*Student Manual.* Retrieved December 5, 2017. http://files
.dnr.state.mn.us/education_safety/safety/instructors/firearms
/instructor_ed_manual.pdf.

National Shooting Sports Foundation. "The Ethical Hunter." Pamphlet, 2006.

National Shooting Sports Foundation. "Firearms Safety Depends on You." Pamphlet, 2006.

National Shooting Sports Foundation. "The Hunter and Conservation." Booklet, 2006.

Peterson, David H. (Hunter Education Instructor, Two Harbors, MN) in discussion with the author, February 2010.

Rinella, Steven. *The Complete Guide to Hunting, Butchering, and Cooking Wild Game.* Vol. 2, *Small Game and Fowl.* New York, NY: Spiegel & Grau, 2015.

Schneck, Marcus. *The North American Hunter's Handbook.* Philadelphia, PA: Running Press, 1991.

Smith, Richard P. *Hunting Rabbits & Hares: The Complete Guide to North America's Favorite Small Game.* Harrisburg, PA: Stackpole Books, 1986.

Sternberg, Dick. *Upland Game Birds.* Minnetonka, MN: Cy Decosse, 1995.

Tarrant, Bill. *The Field & Stream Upland Bird Hunting Handbook.* Guilford, CT: Lyons Press, 1999.

U.S. Fish and Wildlife Service. "Migratory Bird Harvest Information Program (HIP)." January 22, 2016. http://www.fws.gov/hip.

# INDEX

# ABOUT THE AUTHORS

Xina M. Uhl has written numerous educational books for young people, in addition to textbooks, teacher's guides, lessons, and assessment questions. She has tackled subjects including sports, history, biographies, technology, and health concerns. Although she has friends and family who hunt, she shoots animals only through her camera lens. Her blog details her publications as well as interesting facts and the occasional cat picture.

Judy Monroe Peterson is married to an avid hunter who has more than fifty years of hunting experience. She has earned two master's degrees and is the author of many educational books for young people. Currently, she is a writer and editor of K–12 and post–high school curriculum materials on a variety of subjects, including biology, life science, and the environment.

# ABOUT THE CONSULTANT

Benjamin Cowan has over twenty years of both big game and small game hunting experience. In addition to being an avid hunter, Cowan is also a member of many conservation organizations. He currently resides in west Tennessee.

# PHOTO CREDITS